THE PENGUIN POETS

NEW VOLUME

The three poets represented in this anthology, Adrian Henri, Roger McGough and Brian Patten, were part of the 'pop' poetry movement of the sixties and they became popularly known as the 'Liverpool Poets'. Their poetry, irreverent and full of life, reflected the mood of freedom expressed during that period; in contrast with traditional poetry, their poems were accessible to a wider audience.

Since then each has continued as a practising poet and all three have successfully published many verse collections. Through television and radio appearances and public readings of their work they have helped to bring poetry to a new popularity. *New Volume* is the poets' own selection of their best work after *The Mersey Sound* and illustrates how each poet's writing has matured since that time, but their continued concern for contemporary society is still evident in this new anthology.

D1638661

New Volume

Adrian Henri
Roger McGough
Brian Patten

PENGUIN BOOKS

Penguin Books Ltd, Harmondsworth, Middlesex, England
Penguin Books, 40 West 23rd Street, New York, New York 10010, U.S.A.
Penguin Books Australia Ltd, Ringwood, Victoria, Australia
Penguin Books Canada Ltd, 2801 John Street, Markham, Ontario, Canada L3R 1B4
Penguin Books (N.Z.) Ltd, 182–190 Wairau Road, Auckland 10, New Zealand

This selection first published 1983
Copyright © Penguin Books Ltd, 1983
All rights reserved

Made and printed in Great Britain by
Cox & Wyman Ltd, Reading
Set in Palatino by
Rowland Phototypesetting Ltd
Bury St Edmunds, Suffolk

Contents

Adrian Henri

Roger McGough

Brian Patten

Acknowledgements

The poems by Adrian Henri are taken from the following book, to whose publisher acknowledgement is due: 'Death in the Suburbs', 'Autumn Leaving', 'Spring Poem', 'Incident at Longueville', 'Girl Bathing', 'Words Without a Story', 'Red Card', 'A Song in April', 'Short Poems', 'Night Carnation', 'Any Prince to Any Princess' from *From the Loveless Motel*, 1980, Jonathan Cape Ltd. For the rest of the poems acknowledgement is due to the author.

The poems by Roger McGough are taken from the following books, to whose publisher acknowledgement is due: 'I Don't Like the Poems', 'The Birderman', 'The Scarecrow', 'There Was a Knock on the Door. It was the Meat.', 'You and I', 'Noah's Arc', 'Waving at Trains' from *Waving at Trains*, 1982, Jonathan Cape Ltd; 'Pantomime Poem', 'a cat, a horse and the sun', 'There are fascists', '40 – Love', 'Head Injury', 'P.C. Plod at the Pillar Box' from *After the Merrymaking*, 1971, Jonathan Cape Ltd; 'Apostrophe', 'First Day at School' from *In the Glassroom*, 1976, Jonathan Cape Ltd; 'George and the Dragonfly', 'Crusader', 'The Identification' from *Gig*, 1973, Jonathan Cape Ltd; 'Poem for a Dead Poet', 'The Horse's Mouth', 'The Lake', 'Vegetarians', 'Blazing Fruit', '"Take a poem, Miss Smith."', 'The Rot', 'Mouth' from *Holiday on Death Row*, 1979, Jonathan Cape Ltd.

The poems by Brian Patten are taken from the following books, to whose publisher acknowledgement is due: 'A Blade of Grass', 'Simple Lyric', 'The Stolen Orange', 'A Drop of Unclouded Blood', 'Sometimes It Happens', 'On Time For Once' from *Vanishing Trick*, 1976, George Allen & Unwin Ltd; 'The Right Mask', 'Friends', 'Ghost Culture', 'The True Confessions of a Manuscript Sniffer', 'Proclamation from the New Minister of Culture', 'In the High-Rise Alice Dreams of Wonderland', 'Frogs in the Wood', 'Waves' from *Grave Gossip*, 1979, George Allen & Unwin Ltd; 'Someone Coming Back', 'The Literary Gathering', 'Her Song', 'It is Time to Tidy Up Your Life', 'January Gladsong', 'Interruption at the Opera House', 'Spring Song', 'Albatross Ramble', 'Tristan, Waking in his Wood, Panics' from *The Irrelevant Song*, 1971, George Allen & Unwin Ltd; 'Ode on Celestial Music', 'You Come to Me Quiet as Rain Not Yet Fallen' from *Notes to the Hurrying Man*, 1969, George Allen & Unwin Ltd; 'A Few Sentences About Beauty', 'The Likelihood' from *Love Poems*, 1981, George Allen & Unwin Ltd.

Note: Some of the poems have been revised since their first publication.

ADRIAN HENRI

Adrian Henri was born at Birkenhead, Cheshire, in 1932. When he was four his family moved to Rhyl, North Wales, where he attended grammar school. From 1950, for ten seasons, he worked in Rhyl fairground, meanwhile studying for a B.A. degree in fine art, which he received from the University of Durham in 1955. He went to live in Liverpool in 1957 and worked as scenic artist at the Playhouse before holding various teaching jobs. He became interested in poetry performance in 1961, when he first met Roger McGough and Brian Patten. From 1967 to 1970 he led the poetry/rock group 'Liverpool Scene' and was a member of the roadshow 'Grimms' between 1971 and 1973. Since 1970 he has been a freelance poet/painter/singer/songwriter and lecturer and has toured extensively in Europe and elsewhere, including the United States and Canada. His paintings have been exhibited widely, including six John Moores Liverpool exhibitions, and he has had several one-man shows. He was President of the Liverpool Academy of Arts from 1972 to 1981 and President of the Merseyside Arts Association from 1978 to 1980. He lives and works in Liverpool.

His poetry books include *Tonight at Noon* (1968), *City* (1969), *Autobiography* (1971), *The Best of Henri* (1975), *City Hedges* (1977), *From the Loveless Motel* (1980) and *Penny Arcade* (1983). His poems are included in the anthologies *The Liverpool Scene* (1967), *British Poets of Our Time* (1970) and *The Oxford Book of Twentieth-Century Verse* (1973). Other publications include a novel, *I Want* (with Nell Dunn), *Environment and Happenings* (Thames & Hudson World of Art series, 1974) and a story for children, *Eric the Punk Cat*. Among his plays are *I Wonder* (with Michael Kustow), *Yesterday's Girl* (for Granada television, 1973) and, with Nell Dunn, an adaptation of *I Want* (1983).

Death in the Suburbs

The end of the world will surely come
in Bromley South or Orpington

morning in the suburbs:
sunlight thrown like a blanket
over pink-and-white vistas
villas detached and undetached
islanded with flowering cherry,
stone ravens guard the gateposts
the roof left unguarded,
each man's garden a province unto itself
linked only by birdsong
and the tasteful cooing of doves in hedges
magnolia-petals on deep lawns
little clouds of white and purple round rockeries
frozen veils of appleblossom round every doorway.

the earth
moves
sudden
tiny snowstorms of cherryblossom
a black cat runs apprehensive
flocks of starlings
startle from bushes
slow-growing crescendo
of crashing picture-windows
gardens
uprooted
blown pinkandwhite skyhigh
frozen agonies of begonias
held for a moment like a blurred polaroid
lawns flung like carpets

golfclubs potting-sheds wheeled shopping-baskets
hurled into orbit

deepfreezes burst open
prepackaged meals spilling everywhere
invitations to whist-drives coffee-mornings
letters to long-haired sons at campus universities
never to be delivered
pinboards posters of Che Guevara stereo systems
continental quilts rows of neat lettuces
blameless chihuahuas au pair girls
still wet from dreams of Italian waiters
mothers-in-law bullfight trophies sensible wooden toys
whirled helpless in a vortex
rockeries like asteroids
blizzards of appleblossom
against the April sunlight

villa after villa
flickers off like television
birdsounds
blur into the silence
like a vacuum
heaps of white entrails
nestling amid lilies-of-the-valley
ripple like tarmac
gravel chatters the crazy dance of pavingstones
whole avenues implode
gantries and railway bridges
quiet sidings
engulfed by avalanches of privet and hawthorn
waves of chalk earth flecked with hemlock- and nettle-roots
burying commuter-stations.

far away,
the first distant ripples
flutter dovecots
disturb the pigeons

roosting in oasthouses
weekend cottages
doff their thatch to the sky
mountaintops tumble like cumuli
gales of earth
ravage through ryefields
pylons tremble like seismographs
cries of children
circling like seagulls
echo the distance

a
solitary
picnicker
sitting on a breakwater
above the red, flint-strewn beach
hears the distant thunder
as clifftops crumble
looks up from the light scumbling the silver water
to see the horizon catch fire
showers of small stones
smell of uprooted samphire
the last slice of ham a packet of biscuits the small black
clip away unseen   notebook
as the concrete rears vertical
his ears' last echo
the cries of lost sea-birds
one drifting pink petal
catches the dying sunlight.

Hostage

(In memoriam Ulrike Meinhof)

Urban Guerilla
you burst into me
machinegunned
the old poems
stationed at the door
for just such a contingency
made off
with my heart
in the getaway car
despite
a desperate chase
by police in armoured cars
held it to ransom
demanding
nothing less than total involvement.

That night
a bloodless revolution
statues of the old regime
toppled in the streets
victory-fires
lit on every hillside.

Now,
in the final shootout
you fight on alone
at the window of the blazing house
I a voluntary hostage
bewildered
listen to the howl
of approaching squad-cars
taste

the stench of gas-grenades
as the masked militiamen
burst
into the room
wonder
if I'll miss you.

Citysong

angel
dark angel
constant as seasons
infrequent as words
old rainbow midnight
remembered at dawn
breath of wings
on the morning pillow
waking
with dreams in your eyes
fragments of lost conversations
on your lips

Red
Queen of my heart
locked
in the Tower
your willing victim
rivers of faces
not hearing my cries

barges
tug at the tides
helpless I drown
warehouse and Ionic column
down
before my eyes

fireweed
on demolition sites
butterfly
beneath the breaker's hammer
sing for me

Red
Queen
of my heart
mistress of my city
lady of the river

you give me

rainbows
riversides
mountains

I give you

fragments of broken dreams
bustickets
torn snapshots

You send me
anthems
psalms
symphonies

I send you
stammered words
shared bedtime-stories
failed songs
trailing away
night into day . . .

waking
with the key to the woods
black cat lost
in pink-and-white flowers

night into day
Sunday churches penetrate the sky
July fifes and drums
in the William-and-Mary streets

night into day
meeting at morning
leaving at evening

night into day
soft weeds sway
in the river's fastness

night into day
down into darkness
drowning in sunlight

lady
O lady
day into midnight

last breath
on the morning pillow

silent words

forgotten seasons

angel

dark angel

sudden wings
as the clouds
close about us.

Autumn Leaving

1

dead leaves
drift through your words
cold winds
blow between sentences
eddy between paragraphs
wet leaves flat
in the backyard of our love.

I am fed up with you hanging out your words
on the washing-line of my life
my dirty linen for your public

between
between your
wet alleyways your dead
wasteland trees
not growing in the lamplight
dark spaces between the lines
and your words don't tell
how our city is empty and
how for seven years
bound to you syllable by syllable
street by street paragraph by paragraph.

I shall no longer wait for the telephone
to tell me the poems you write for others
nor wash your lies from the kitchen floor

our love
as silent as words
as noisy as backyards
as desolate as sentences.

I shall no longer clean this bedroom
other women's words snug beneath your pillow
the bedclothes stiff with adjectives

away from you
here
in this abandoned valley
drifts of dead nouns
drowned verbs
hills spread apart
rich orange-red slopes
brazen to the sky
to the sound of you still
on the tip of my tongue.

I will no longer
Hoover the corners of our life
nor
lie back and let you
bury your words in me

words apart
and only the streetlights between us
waiting these years
between lamplight and morning.

2

Onion in December

an onion in December
layers of words
plump with unshed tears

and stored sunlight
waiting on the shelf
for your winter knife.

3

Spring Ending

and
tomorrow
students
will lay gentle flowers
on the bloodstained pavement
where our relationship died
last night.

4

Full and Frank

At summit conferences
we argue
about custody of the deodorant
and visiting hours for the cat
at weekends. Fair shares
of the wallpaper
and last year's European Cup programme.

A pillowcase
a dusty sugar pig
and two dog-eared cookery books
lurk
on the agenda.

Our tears
wait
under Any Other Business.

5

Morning Two

waking
and reaching out for you
in the curtained light
the empty space beside me
throbs the stump of our love
a phantom limb
beneath the bedclothes.

6

Robins

Christmas cards come
addressed to the two of us
I wonder
shall I tear them in half?
send you the robins?
keep the holly?

7

Cenotaph

In this corner
of a foreign girl
I suddenly remember how
the smell of T.C.P.
used to excite me
nightly,
how
we came close and then slept.

Now
at dawn
a bugle sounds
I whisper excuses

and, leaving,
lay a wreath upon the pillow.

'At the going down of the drawers,
And in the morning,
We will remember them.'

8

Pressing the wings of butterflies for paper
I write you poems at midnight.
Their small, still, silent voices
Echo my words.

from 'Autobiography'

1   *Part One   1932–51*

flags and bright funnels of ships
walking with my mother over the Seven Bridges
and being carried home too tired
frightened of the siren on the ferryboat
or running down the platform on the Underground
being taken over the river to see the big shops at Christmas
the road up the hill from the noisy dockyard
and the nasty smell from the tannery you didn't like going
                    past
steep road that made your legs tired
up the hill from the Co-op the sweetshop the
                    blue-and-white-tiled pub
Grandad's allotment on the lefthand side
behind the railings curved at the top
cobblestone path up the middle to the park
orderly rows of bean canes   a fire burning   sweetpeas tied
                    up on strings
up to Our House
echoing flagyard entry between the two rows of houses
brick buttresses like lumps of cheese against the backyard
                    walls
your feet clang and echo on the flags as you run the last few
                    yards
pulling your woolly gloves off
shouting to show Grandad what you've just been bought
him at the door tall like the firtree in the park
darkblue suit gleaming black boots shiny silver watch chain
striped shirt no collar on but always a collarstud
heavy grey curled moustache that tickles when he picks you
                    up to kiss you

sometimes shouting angry frightening you
till you see the laughter in his countryman's blue eyes

2

round redbrick doorway
yellow soapstone step cleaned twice a week
rich darkred linopattern in the polished lobby
front room with lace runners and a piano that you only go in
                on Sundays
or when someone comes to tea
Uncle Bill asleep in his chair coming in smelling of beer and
                horses
limping with the funny leg he got in the war
Grandma always in a flowered apron
the big green-and-red parrot frightening you with his sudden
                screeches
the two little round enamelled houses on either side of the
                fireplace
big turquoise flowered vase in the middle
the grate shining blackleaded cooking smell from the oven
                next to it

big black sooty kettle singing on the hob
fireirons in the hearth
foghorns and hooters
looking out of the kitchen window
seeing the boats on the bright river
and the cranes from the dockyards

3

coming back the taxidriver doesn't know where the street is
the allotments at the foot of the hill
gone now
great gaunt terraces of flats

scarred with graffiti
instead
the redbrick houses tiny falling apart
the whitewashed backyard
where you could smell lilyofthevalley through the privethedge
round the tiny garden
on your way to the lavatory at the end
empty dirty overgrown now
backdoor banging in the wind
grandmother grandfather both dead in hospital
one windowpane broken dirty lace curtain flapping
the funny little flights of steps
the secret passages in the park
pink sandstone steps overhung with trees up the side of the
hill
overgrown or demolished
the big seacaptain's house where I used to go for a present
every Christmas
forgotten
remembering
lying in bed
in the dark crying listening to my mother and father argue
wind banging a shutter
indoors somewhere
dead eyes looking out from flyblown photographs
empty mirrors reflecting the silence

4

RHYL SANDS:
your vision swept clear and bright by the wind that's wiping
away the stormclouds
beach low and empty   pale blue sky   seagulls and one dog
near the horizon
pebbles underfoot as clear as the wallpaper in seaside cafés
somewhere out at sea, a rainbow
the sad peeling offseason colours of arcades and kiosks

David Cox's 'Rhyl Sands' a tiny gem burning quietly in dirty
                        Manchester
ghostly echoes of last season's chip-papers in the drifting sand

6

carrying my gasmask to school every day
buying savings stamps
remembering my National Registration Number
(ZMGM/136/3 see I can *still* remember it)
avoiding Careless Talk Digging for Victory
looking for German spies everywhere
Oh yes, I did my bit for my country that long dark winter,
me and Winston and one or two others,
wearing my tin hat whenever possible
singing 'Hang out the Washing on the Siegfried Line'
aircraft-recognition charts pinned to my bedroom wall
the smell of paint on toy soldiers
doing paintings of Spitfires and Hurricanes, Lancasters and
                        Halifaxes
always with a Heinkel or a Messerschmitt plunging helplessly
                        into the sea in the background
pink light in the sky from Liverpool burning 50 miles away
the thunder of daylight flying fortresses high overhead
                        shaking the elderberry-tree
bright barrageballoons flying over the docks
morning curve of the bay seen from the park on the hill
after coming out of the air raid shelter
listening for the 'All Clear' siren
listening to Vera Lynn Dorothy Lamour Allen Jones and
                        The Andrews Sisters
clutching my father's hand tripping over the unfamiliar kerb
I walk over every day
in the blackout

7

walking to the spring wood now a muddy buildersyard
footpaths then mysterious trackless intrepid
now suburban bungalowstreets gravel and tarmac
where the churnedup mud horsedung and puddles were
the woods alive with primrose and milkwort
wood-anemone and bright hawthorn
now a haven for gnomes and plastic waterfalls

12

sunlight on long grass
old lace curtains draped over raspberry canes
plump gooseberries cobwebbed in the shadows
the smell of lilac and woodfires burning
remembering the day I walked five miles to draw the waterfall
then found my pen was empty and bought a postcard with my
                          last sixpence
and had to walk home
the postcard still pinned on my studio wall
frozen water falling white blood from a giant's side
walking after cocoa and buns and hearing of a poet's death on
                          the radio
alone in the vast sad hospital
cowparsley patterning the hedges
light spilt like paint through the leaves

13

deep rosepetals on a close-cropt lawn
the scent of clover lying close to the earth
envious of the coolness under the green rosebush
a sad young poet thinking of her eyes the colour of shadows
                          under the sycamores
shadows and a myriad insects creep in the tangled grasses
in the evening sunlight
filled with the sound of a thousand departing motorcoaches

14

remembering
the sudden pangs at corners
glimpsing the laughter of happy couples in the street
flat moonbranch shadows on the pavement
under a summer moon
or winter lamplight
nightwalks through the purgatory of half-built housingestates
the last-minute shifting of a cushion
for the seduction-scene that never takes place
for the waiting at the end of the privetlane
for the person who never comes

15

sad
boy-to-be-poet
head full of words
understood by no one
walking the dog
through the midnight bungaloworld
built over the
countryside
of his dreams

Metropolis

(for David Gascoyne)

1

gravelponds along long lines
fruit-trees heavy in the autumn sunlight
disturbed only by the falling brickdust
and the distant roar of engines in the morning air.

blackberries glinting in the sunlight
poised against the sky toppling into enormous pits
hayfields troutstreams drystone walls
falling tumbling rolling before the gleaming blades
squashed hedgehogs dying owls rabbits screaming
grass and tiny bodies tangled in the clay
before the march of giant earthmovers.

O stars trees ponds
tornup roots of farmhouses
gape into the mist
allnight roar of a thousand cementmixers
acetylene lights flooding the sky.

2

apocalypse of weirs foaming into polluted canals
endless landscape of factoryfields
chimneys belching dark into the distance
all roads home gleaming far away silver seen briefly through
the drifting clouds.

vast reactors megatheriums of pylons
tangled webs of cables blotting out the light
save for bright sodium-lights above the rushing expressways

flyover cloverleaf underpass
one way only every which way
roadways layered up into the darkness.

3

concrete empty electric hallways
echoing with the sound of Muzak
shopfronts still boarded shuttering still on the pillars
scaffolding everywhere through the haze
glass towers into the sky
acres of polished tables boardroom carpet
empty halls of computers and filing cabinets.

endless escalators vistas of plump thighs
nylon curved crammed tight with bursting flesh
tight glimpsed whitecotton secrets
soft female smell in the secret darkness
nerveless fingers immobile on trains
touching the warm imagined places
vistas of pink nipples haloed through delicate lace
disappearing out of the corners of the eyes.

NIGHT The neon landscape
the soft purr of skysigns switching on at evening
like the roosting of longdead pigeons
nightlong litany of hammers and rockdrills
green light flickering from the wall-to-wall telescreens.

4

huge bridges majestic arches
spanning the longdead beds of rivers
dried pramwheels rusty cans bones of dead animals
stagnant pools rainbowed with oil
where fishes once swarmed.

limitless vistas of bungalows and tower-flats
behind the highways
obscured constantly by the gathering darkness
ceaseless flashing of commutercars under the yellow lights
gaping mouths of endless tunnels
gleaming silver trains swish and rattle into blackness
old videotapes of trees played rushingly past the empty
                              windows
stereo birdsong through the airconditioned silence.

A Song for A. E. Housman

I walk the lanes of Wenlock
And dream about the night
Where every leaf is shrivelled
And every berry bright

In Wenlock Town the drink goes down
The laughter flows like wine
In Wenlock Town the leaves are brown
And you're no longer mine

Day turns to night in Wenlock
Laughter to early tears
Down by the hill I follow still
The path we walked this year

Come let it snow on Wenlock
Fall down and cover me
Happy I was in Wenlock
Happy no more I'll be.

Don't Look

Don't look in my eyes, then
look at the dragonflies
glittering look at the river

Don't listen to my words
listen to the crickets,
loud in the hayfield listen to the water

Don't touch me
don't feel my lips my body
feel the earth alive with sedges
trefoil valerian feel the sunlight

My lady,
these things I bring you
don't see only know
a landscape in your body
a river in my eyes

Butterfly

(for Carol Ann Duffy)

cry
for the butterfly
in your warm hand
hard light
on the threadbare tapestry of my wings
rainbow dust
left on the loved lines
of your palm

cry
with me
helpless
pinned against
stark white
black writing

sing
of your gift
for your lover
as I fall
flicker against your feet

sing
as I die
caught between intricate syllables
your song
pierce my body
butterfly
flutters
at the foot of the page
tiny rainbow
dies for your song
in the evening sunlight.

Epilogue

(for D.H.L.)

Autumn
and leaves swirl at the roadside
splatter on windscreens
summer hopes gone
fears for the dark
the long night ahead
light ebbing to the slow horizon

'Autumn,
The falling fruit,
The long journey,'

Prepare for the dark
O bring it home with you
tuck it into bed
welcome him into your hearth
into your heart
the familiar stranger at the evening fireside

Wind howls in the trees
and toads curl into beds of leaves
night moves into day
moths into velvet
hedges brown with dying willow-herb

Open your door to the dark
the evening snow drift in unheeded
light dies from the sky
gather the stranger close on the pillow

seeds lie buried
safe under hedgerows
gather him to you
O gather him to you

Take the dark stranger
Cold under blankets
Gather O Gather
Alone in the darkness.

ADRIAN HENRI

Poem for Liverpool 8

LIVERPOOL 8:
blaze of trumpets from basement recordplayers
loud guitars in the afternoon
knowing every inch of little St Bride St
brightgreen patches of mildew redpurple bricks stained ochre
                                        plaster
huge hearts names initials kisses painted on backdoors
tiny shop with a lightbulb in the window
Rodney St pavement stretching to infinity
Italian garden by the priest's house
seen through the barred doorway on Catherine St
pavingstones worn smooth for summer feet
St James Rd my first home in Alan's flat
shaken intolerable by Cathedral bells on Sundays
Falkner Sq. Gardens heaped with red leaves to kick in autumn
shuttered yellowgreen with sunlight
noisy with children's laughter in summer
black willows into cold mist
bushes railings pillowed with snow in winter
Gambier Terrace loud Beatle guitars from the first floor
Sam painting beckoning phantoms hiding behind painted
                                        words bright colours
in the flooded catfilled basement
pigeons disappearing at eyelevel into the mist
hopscotch-figures vomitstains under my morning feet
Granby St bright bazaars for aubergines and coriander
Blackburne House girls laughing at bus-stops in the afternoon
Blackburne Place redbrick Chirico tower rushing back after
                                        love at dinnertime
drunk jammed in the tiny bar in The Cracke
drunk in the crowded cutglass Philharmonic
drunk in noisy Jukebox O'Connor's

smiling landlord on the doorstep huge in shirtsleeves and
braces

LIVERPOOL 8:
now a wasteland
murdered by planners not German bombers
crossed by empty roads
drunken lintels falling architraves
Georgian pediments peeling above toothless windows
no Mrs Boyne laughing in the Saturdaynight Greek chipshop
the tumbledown graveyard under the Cathedral
where we kissed behind willowtrees
bulldozed into tidy gardens
huge tornup roots of trees
pink sandstone from uprooted walls glittering in pale sunlight
no happy dirtyfaced children
littering the sidestreets
only a distant echo of their laughter
across the bonfire fireengine debris.

Scenes from the Permissive Society

1 There were no survivors from the dawn raid . . .
(for Richard Hill)

Soldiers of love:
returning at dawn
shock-troops
in the sex-war
dropped
2 doors away
no prisoners taken
cyanide button sewn onto lapel
excuses timed
with a self-destruct mechanism
activated
at the first sign of tears.

2 Poem to be printed on a pair of paper panties

Throw these away in the morning
Like the things we said last night
Words that go bump in the darkness
Crumpled and stained in the light

Promises made with our bodies
Dropped in the bin by the day
Look for the signs of our loving
Carefully hide them away

Straighten the folds in the bedclothes
Smooth out the pillow we shared
Tidied away in the corner
Along with our last lying words.

3

I want a love
as intimate as feminine deodorant
As easily disposed of
as paper underwear
As fresh as
the last slice of sliced bread
As instant as
flavour-rich coffee granules
As necessary as
money
Available
on demand
A love
as glossy
double-spread
full-colour
full-frontal
as a Bunny-girl
(and the only key
belongs to me)

I want a
Number One
Smooth creamy
Hi-speed
Cross-your-Heart
Getaway
Cool as a
Cosy-Glo
Fingertip control
Throwaway
Here today
Never pay
Any way
love.

ADRIAN HENRI

Spring Poem

'be quiet say nothing
except the street be full of stars'
                    – Pablo Picasso, translated by David Gascoyne

except the canals be full of evening
and our hands full of lamplight
the sky the colour of irises

except the tomorrow sunlight fill the room
pale as your discarded underwear
and the streets be full of the taste of your body

except we open the door in the forest
and step out into the hallway
your eyes a prayer without end in the darkness

except
that the tides of the year will move through the sand
beneath the houses

beneath the plane trees, the bicycles
beneath the cobblestones, the sea
beneath my body,
your body.

The Triumph of Death

Thunder in the dark at Adrian Henri's . . .

1

birdsong
dropping into space between the sodium-lights
footsteps echo on the wet yellow pavement
down the hill lights of the unknown hometown
bright across the river

First faint chords drift in from the orchestra
woodwinds high in the air
light from the evening sun catching the river
dockyards at the end of the street
flicker with the first smudges of flame
sudden skull-head peering from round the street-corner
seen for a moment from the top of the street
shopping-bag in hand
white beckoning skeleton hand unnoticed behind the
parked cars
darkling sky clouding the silver water

2

Fanfare of French Horns:
cars pile relentless into each other at trafficlights
grinning skeletal policemen
ride ambulances over pedestrians
klaxon-horns blaring

MUSIC FULL UP:
strings brass tympani
hoarse screams of owls from parks
despairing wail of sirens from sinking ferryboats
roar of exploding oil-tanks
walls of flame round abandoned tankers
figures of men broken on wheels against the lurid sky

high
above
squadron upon squadron
of dark figures
wheel triumphantly
row derisively amongst the carnage
salmon leap despairingly from the boiling waters

3

images from the haunted screen:

in the deserted cinema
a trapped usherette
smashes shattering the waxen mask
grinning hideous face beneath
football-crowds melting like waxworks
faces running marble eyeballs fallen from sockets
rooftops at crazy angles
dark figure in at the bedroom window
classrooms burst into flame
a skeleton exposes his rotting pelvis
to the helpless gaze of a class of schoolgirls

4

typists shopgirls errandboys
scream hopelessly
run towards ornamental gardens
from the falling buildings

white mocking figures insolently riding the debris
neat gardens in St James' Cemetery
torn apart
wreathed and cellophaned flowers tumbled aside
as gravecloths burst into the light
white blinking stumbling figures
queue at the gravemouths

black crows perch on the remains of department stores
dying seagulls splattered helpless against the sky
vultures wait on the Cathedral tower
busloads of darkrobed skeleton figures
raping laughing dancing singing
a revolving door spins unheeded
the hotel lounge littered with corpses

gibbets long as vermin-poles down the middle of streets
mocking roar of music behind the explosions
thunder in the dark
light only from the burning earth
dark dark dark
white bony mocking faces everywhere

5

And you beside me, my morning girl of the shadows
the inscrutable nurse always at the morning bedside
white breasts sprouting naked beneath your black cloak
head thrown back swirls of rivermist in your hair
take me fold me forever in your warm darkness
suck the cold life from my willing veins
lost in a final dark embrace

black barge straining waiting at the riverbank.

Two Lullabys

1

Here is a poem written on the clouds for you
When white bodies dance in suburban gardens
Accompanied only by the sound of lawnmowers
Champagne pouring into empty swimming-pools
Here is a poem written on the clouds for you

Here is a poem written on the sky for you
On the very last day
When skulls and hummingbirds crowd the beaches like
                                        deckchairs
Seagulls singing their final requiem
Here is a poem written on the sky for you

Here is a poem written in the air for you
When the flood is over
And pigs are left dangling in the treetops
Valleys overturned and rivers upended
Here is a poem written in the air for you

Here is a poem written on the clouds for you
When the poets are gone and the poems forgotten
When a new earth blooms
And the dying heart pumps a song of welcome
Here is a poem written on the clouds for you.

2

Woken and then lulled by the seagulls
Sleep till the sea-fret rolls by
Turn on your pillow till morning
Back to the opening sky

Sleep though the dreams may come crowding
Like mists across the bay
Night-birds will hover above you
Cry to the echoing day

Sleep though the aeroplanes lull you
Dull through the evening skies
Sleep with the seabirds for guardians
Distances lost in their eyes

Sandpipers wade on the marshes
Curlews awake on the plain
Turn to the cobblestone sunlight
Wake to the morning again.

An Incident at Longueville

(for John and Ann Willett)

1

It is early afternoon. Late summer sunlight fills the street.
The sound of bells. She waits outside the Café Tellier.
She has been there since the bells in the slate-spired church
last rang. Dark hat, almost like a beret, pulled well
over her eyes. The shadow of the awning of the Café Tellier
falls at an acute angle. She waits with hands in pockets
head down does not see the shadow nor hear the laughter
of the five girls walking arm-in-arm beneath the little railway
                                                        bridge
at the end of the street.

2

Bells again. It is le Quinze Août and the town closed
for holiday. Still she waits head down unseeing.
The laughing girls have long since gone. Baked mud and brick
                                                        walls
reflect the heat. The gravel of the forecourt in front of the Café
                                                        Tellier
stirs beneath her foot. The shadow of the awning has moved,
imperceptibly. The crossing-bell and the heavy breath of an
                                                        approaching
train. The foot turned out towards us taps unconsciously on
                                                        the gravel
to its rhythm.

3

Catching her breath slightly from the uphill walk,
too hot in the thick coat with the fur collar, her

tight shoes resent the cobblestones. She walks into
the Place du Calvaire, then waits in the middle of the little
street
behind the monument. A child watches, incurious,
from outside his garden gate, blue school smock on despite
the feast-day.
In the background a tall fir tree overgrown with ivy. The ochre
walls of wood-framed barns. The shadow of the Cross
falls on the brick wall behind it, the arms a shallow angle
to the single band of yellow brick. Its two metal supports are
shadowed
like a corollary.

4

She stands as before, head down, no longer hearing
or counting the bells. No traffic turns the steep corner
by the Cross. Hands still in pockets, she stares at the base
of the sunbrick wall. She does not see nor think of the frozen
bronze agony
whose harsh shadow shifts yet again as we watch.
Lengthening
shadows in a red-tiled kitchen await her return.
Le Quinze Août, Feast of the Assumption, the festive tables
are ready. Soon she will walk out of the Place du Calvaire.
In the dark forest along the valley a white château dreams.

5

She walks away from us down the Rue de Belgique. The
shadow
outside the Café Tellier has lengthened almost to vertical.
Round the corner by the épicerie trots a white horse,
bridled but not saddled, led by a fat, unsmiling workman,
cigarette and bleus de travail. The man who rides the horse's
back
is made of flowers.

Girl Bathing

You step from the bath
smelling of apples, chestnuts, avocadoes
breath of pine-needles about your feet
Deep Rich Smooth Relaxing
smiling Pomona
a fruit-stall on a frosty morning
your laughing fingers will bring joy
to the waiting millions in the bedroom.

Ladies, Lords and Golden Rings
Ninepenny Geese and Sevenpenny Swans
All in a Paper Peartree

Pollyanna of the bedsitters,
Rebecca of Sunnybrooke Terrace,
still trailing clouds of cucumber and rosemary
you will step out and into the morning
like the sun over winter rooftops.

Words Without a Story

(from 'Geschichte Ohne Worte':
60 woodcuts by Franz Masereel)

1

In the city we meet. Incurious lightning flickers in the
distance.

2

Almost meeting in the country, you turn away from me.

3

Hand on heart I swear my devotion: you turn from my noisy
streets to your silent arbour.

4

I light candles, monstrances for you: you cast your eyes
downwards.

5

Wise as a shepherd I counsel patience, reason. You touch the
cat rubbing against your leg.

6

I speak these words for you, the sunrise spread like a peacock
behind me;

7

I bring gold and precious stones bright as the rising moon;

8

I fall to my knees in supplication; ignoring all these things,
you watch the birds in the garden.

9

Wildly I implore you: you bury your face in a rose.

10

By candlelight I consider other strategies. You hesitate.

11

Beneath the gaze of the servile waiter, you sweep away from
the table.

12

I follow you with bouquets, telegrams. You walk into your
flower garden.

13

I set off ecstasies of fireworks. You cover your eyes.

14

On the steps of the Bourse I juggle bright coins: you pause a
moment.

15

I weep in the jungle. You turn, indifferent as a tiger.

16

Distraught I implore you in the city. You step behind a barrier of concrete.

17

Feigning nonchalance, I propose a sophisticated arrangement. The parrot mimes your departure.

18

I am photographed amongst orchids, guinea-fowl, cassowaries. You are unimpressed.

19

I step from my carriage, lamplight gleaming on my well-brushed hat. You are equally unimpressed.

20

In the dismal swamp I step out in rags, touch your dress. You do not notice me.

21

In the farmyard I confront you, tear my clothes away.

22

In the orchard I display myself erect before you. You peep between your hands.

23

At the turn of the stair I pause, perplexed. You are preoccupied.

24

At the circus I juggle bright balls, turn cartwheels. You permit
yourself a smile.

25

Frantic I turn the world upside down, then stand on my head
for you. Still you do not react.

26

I bring back rainbows, planets, nebulae, strange interstellar
creatures. You seem amused.

27

Emboldened I dance fandangoes, tarantellas. Hired musicians
play in the orange-groves.

28

I sing the song I wrote for you, my voice rivals the blackbird's.
You cover your ears.

29

Sweat pouring from me, I raise whole officeblocks. You step
neatly from the picture.

30

In the midst of starving millions I entreat you. You are remote
as tall factories.

31

My limbs aching, we meet in the midnight churchyard.
You are demure, flirtatious.

32

Where the cross looms at the junction of seven roads you will
not wait for me.

33

By the railway-line I slip my hands boldly beneath your arms.

34

In the alley where the cats howl their love I touch for a
moment the warmth beneath your dress.
You slap my hand.

35

From the very flames themselves I cry out to you. You shrug
your shoulders.

36

Where the willows rise urgent as my desire I am bold as the
wind. You touch your breast for a moment.

37

My love is fierce as a tempest. Fish flap in the trees and tritons
play beneath a dark sun. You are estranged again.

38

In the dark wood where the poison mushrooms blow I step
out, knife in hand. You call my bluff.

39

I throw away the knife, weep my contrition. A hart appears,
magic light streams between his horns. You
do not see him.

40

On the steps of the Cathedral I kneel. The bells cannot call you
back.

41

Doglike, I crouch in Skid Row. The scent of your petticoats
brushes past me.

42

I throw my filthy arms around your dainty feet. You call a
policeman.

43

As you kick me aside I think: this is the first time she has
touched me.

44

The drunken city flies back at crazy angles. You permit a
flutter of your fan as you pass.

45

Reeling I perform a hopeless jig. You do not even see me.

46

Like a depraved mountebank I leap, cavort. There is only a
distant echo of your laughter.

47

I will throw myself into the moonhaunted sea. The laughter of
the drowned echoes your disdain.

48

I step onto the balcony. The traffic roars beneath. Perhaps now
you will listen.

49

As I prepare the rope the black carriage rumbles past. Crows
and the sound of bells fill the sky. You hesitate.

50

In the potter's field the bony hand an inch away from mine,
you slowly turn.

51

The dead themselves crowd to see us as you step towards me,
sudden light in your eyes.

52

Your lips on mine, all earth and heaven forgotten.

53

Impatient you fling your clothes away. They fall like petals
your body pale as sandalwood.

54

Your eyes closed we roll amongst galaxies. I am aware of a
distant star.

55

Back on earth I dress myself wearily. Naked and bestial you
twine yourself around me.

56

Your eyes your dripping body demand. Clouds fill the sky.
I cannot hide the distance in me.

57

Tears fall between your hands. At the window I wait for the
rain to stop.

58

You spread yourself before me the white breasts the once-
imagined darkness between your thighs. I move
away, quietly.

59

As I slip finally from the picture it shows you slumped against
the earth. Your tears are bright in the sunrise.

60

Now only
THE END
is between us.

Red Card

Right from the off,
straight into your penalty area
a quick one-two and it was all over
bar the shouting. Easy
Easy sang the terraces.
Half-time: I've given you a hundred per cent
and more. Two down, and I've got it all
to do again.

At the end of the day
the lap of honour. Your ribbons
round the Cup. I am
sick as a parrot. I am
over the moon you tell the cameras,
the waiting millions.
Back home I walk
alone.

A Song in April

(another song for A.E.H.)

The buds of April bursting
Into the flowers of May
Await a cold November
Forgotten in the clay

The lambs of April playing
Are due to die in June
The loves of April laughing
Will come to tears too soon

The loves of April blossom
And last a summer long
Come close, for chill October
Will come to end the song

Come close, my love, and tell me
April will never end
That daffodil like gorse-bush
Will last to the year's end

That lambs will dance for ever
And lovers never part;
Come close upon the pillow
And still my restless heart.

The Dance of Death

autumn to winter:
willowherb turns indigo
against the orange of its going
bonfires in backyards
hold the fitful dusk at bay
flushed childrens' faces
candles in pumpkins
strains of the 'Dies Irae' heard in the distance.

Dancing figures against the fading skyline
bony feet through withered leaves
leaping singing flapping like stormclouds
Death the Magician
conjuring darkness out of daylight
Death and the Lovers
crouching behind the settee peering through the curtains
Death and the Maiden
cold phalanxes of fingers over goosepimpled flesh
probing the warm and secret places
'. . . there will now follow a party political broadcast
on behalf of Death . . . this programme will be shown
on all channels . . .'
Death the Politician
polished white face carefully sipping water
adjusting his fireside manner
DEATH RULES OK·
scrawled on a wall outside the football stadium
Death the Terrorist Death the Avenger
O there is no hiding from the secret bomber
the parcel left unnoticed in the crowded discotheque
Death the Trafficwarden Death the Controller
bodies spilling everywhere

trainsmash or planecrash
carbrakes on tarmac
Death and the Soldier
familiar companion
riding a troop-carrier in camouflage gravecloths
Death and the Boatman
steering the October ferry to Eridanus
Death the Popsinger –
obscene spangled bony limbs gyrating –
Death and the Drunkard
grinning behind the barmaid's smile
Death and the Junkie
kindly refilling the hypodermic
Death and the Priest
mocking laughter from behind the altar
sly white face behind the confessional
Death and the Schoolgirl
cold hand up her gymslip in the autumn park
Death and the Farmer
following the furrow seed falling barren
Death in the Supermarket,
Corner-shop, Greengrocers',
Dance-hall and Waiting-room,
Alehouse and News-stand,
Housewife and Bunnygirl
join in the sarabande
hold hands and dance, dance
as the lightnings whirl
dance, dance, dance to the darkness . . .

eve,
and the Michaelmas moon
rise in the firtrees
last strains of music
heard from the deadlands
November dreams
lost amongst stormclouds.

Short Poems

What Shall We Do With The Drunken Poet?

Thinking of you on a waterbed
Feeling
Seasick with jealousy.

Football Poem/Goodbye Poem

You never wore
cologne.

ADRIAN HENRI

Night Carnation

Night carnation,
asleep in the shadows of your hair,
its blood staining the morning pillow.
Outside the snow breathes, patters
on the window. Within
our warmth, the faint persistent scent
insists. Our love
like a carnation in the dark
stains the night air
with its presence.

Any Prince to Any Princess

August is coming
and the goose, I'm afraid,
is getting fat.
There have been
no golden eggs for some months now.
Straw has fallen well below market price
despite my frantic spinning
and the sedge is,
as you rightly point out,
withered.

I can't imagine how the pea
got under your mattress. I apologize
humbly. The chambermaid has, of course,
been sacked. As has the frog footman.
I understand that, during my recent fact-finding tour
                                  of the Golden River,
despite your nightly unavailing efforts,
he remained obstinately
froggish.

I hope that the Three Wishes granted by the General
                                              Assembly
will go some way towards redressing
this unfortunate recent sequence of events.
The fall in output from the shoe-factory, for example:
no one could have foreseen the work-to-rule
by the National Union of Elves. Not to mention the fact
that the court has been fast asleep
for the last six and a half years.
The matter of the poisoned apple has been taken up
by the Board of Trade: I think I can assure you

the incident will not be
repeated.

I can quite understand, in the circumstances,
your reluctance to let down
your golden tresses. However
I feel I must point out
that the weather isn't getting any better
and I already have a nasty chill
from waiting at the base
of the White Tower. You must see
the absurdity of the situation.
Some of the courtiers are beginning to talk,
not to mention the humble villagers.
It's been three weeks now, and not even
a word.

Princess,
a cold, black wind
howls through our empty palace.
Dead leaves litter the bedchamber;
the mirror on the wall hasn't said a thing
since you left. I can only ask,
bearing all this in mind,
that you think again,

let down your hair,

reconsider.

Morning Song

Of meat and flowers I sing
Butchers and gardeners:

When aware of the body's process
The long journey into red night
The unfamiliar pounding that may cease at any moment
Drift off into the night full of sounds
Ticklings and murmurs, whispers and gurglings

When my mouth
Open against the open world of you
Into the darkness of rosepetals
Continents against white continents
Shudder in perspective

When the curtains are drawn
And you blossom into morning
Eyes unveiled from sleep flower-beds thrown back
White lilies against your hair's vine-leaves
I will rise and moisten the warm wet soil
to perfection:

Of meat and flowers I sing
Butchers and gardeners:
Songs thrown bleeding onto counters
Reaching up to the sun through city backyards.

ROGER McGOUGH

Roger McGough was born in Liverpool in 1937 and educated at St Mary's College and the University of Hull. Following this he taught for three years before entering the pop world as a member of 'The Scaffold' and later of 'Grimms'. Since then he has written for stage and television and has given readings of his work throughout the known world. His books include *Watchwords* (1969), *After the Merrymaking* (1971), *Out of Sequence* (1972), *Gig* (1973), *Sporting Relations* (1974), *In the Glassroom* (1976), *Mr Noselighter* (1977), *Summer with Monika* (1978), *Holiday on Death Row* (1979), *You Tell Me* (with Michael Rosen, 1979), *Unlucky for Some* (1980), *Strictly Private* (editor, 1981), *Waving at Trains* (1982), *The Great Smile Robbery* (1982) and *Sky in the Pie* (1983).

I Don't Like the Poems

I don't like the poems they're making me write
I really don't like them at all
Hierograffiti I don't understand
Scrawled on a hologrammed wall.

They wake me up in the middle of the night
I really don't like them one bit
Dictating mysterious messages
That I am forced to transmit.

Messages with strange metaphors, ass-
onance, similies and the like.
Internal rhymes that chime, and alas
External ones that sometimes don't quite make it.

I don't like the poems they filter through me
Using words I never would use
Like 'filter', 'hierograffiti', 'alien'
I'm enslaved by an alien muse.

*   *   *

And I notice, just lately, at readings
That friends whose work I have known
Unknowingly have started to write
In a similarly haunted tone.
Stumbling over poems we have to recite
In handwriting that isn't our own.

The Birderman

Most weekends, starting in the spring
Until late summer, I spend angling.
Not for fish. I find that far too tame
But for birds, a much more interesting game.

A juicy worm I use as bait
Cast a line into the tree and wait.
Seldom for long (that's half the fun)
A commotion in the leaves, the job's half done.

Pull hard, jerk home the hook
Then reel him in. Let's have a look . . .
A tiny thing, a fledgling, young enough to spare.
I show mercy. Unhook, and toss it to the air.

It flies nestwards and disappears among the leaves
(What man roasts and braises, he too reprieves).
What next? A magpie. Note the splendid tail.
I wring its neck. Though stringy, it'll pass for quail.

Unlike water, the depths of trees are high
So, standing back, I cast into the sky.
And ledger there beyond the topmost bough,
Until threshing down, like a black cape, screams a crow!

Evil creature! A witch in feathered form.
I try to net the dark, encircling storm.
It caws for help. Its cronies gather round
They curse and swoop. I hold my ground.

An infernal mass, a black, horrific army
I'll not succumb to Satan's origami.
I reach into my coat, I've come prepared,
Bring out my pocket scarecrow – Watch out bird!

It's cross-shaped, the sign the godless fear
In a thunderflap of wings they disappear.
Except of course, that one, ungainly kite
Broken now, and quickly losing height.

I haul it in, and with a single blow
Dispatch it to that Aviary below.
The ebb and flow: magpie, thrush, nightingale and crow.
The wood darkens. Time to go.

I pack away the food I've caught
And thankful for a good day's sport
Amble home. The forest fisherman.
And I'll return as soon as I can

To bird. For I'm a birderer. The birderman.

The Scarecrow

The scarecrow is a scarey crow
Who guards a private patch
Waiting for a trespassing
Little girl to snatch

Spitting soil into her mouth
His twiggy fingers scratch
Pulls her down on to the ground
As circling birdies watch

Drags her to his hidey-hole
And opens up the hatch
Throws her to the crawlies
Then double locks the latch

The scarecrow is a scarey crow
Always out to catch
Juicy bits of compost
to feed his cabbage patch

So don't go where the scarecrows are
Don't go there, Don't go there
Don't go where the scarecrows are
Don't go, Don't go . . .

Don't go where the scarecrows are
Don't go there, Don't go there
Don't go where the scarecrows are
Don't go . . .

Pantomime Poem

'HE'S BEHIND YER!'
chorused the children
but the warning came too late.

The monster leaped forward
and fastening its teeth into his neck,
tore off the head.

The body fell to the floor
'MORE' cried the children

'MORE, MORE, MORE

MORE

MC

Poem for a Dead Poet

He was a poet he was.
A proper poet.
He said things
that made you think
and said them nicely.
He saw things
that you or I
could never see
and saw them clearly.
He had a way
with language.
Images flocked around
him like birds,
St Francis, he was,
of the words. Words?
Why he could almost make 'em talk.

a cat, a horse and the sun

a cat mistrusts the sun
keeps out of its way
only where sun and shadow meet
it moves

a horse loves the sun
it basks all day
snorts
and beats its hooves

the sun likes horses
but hates cats
that is why it makes hay
and heats tin roofs

Apostrophe

'twould be nice to be
an apostrophe
floating
above an s
hovering
like a paper kite
in between the its
eavesdropping, tiptoeing
high about the thats
an inky comet
spiralling
the highest tossed
of hats

First Day at School

A millionbillionwillion miles from home
Waiting for the bell to go. (To go where?)
Why are they all so big, other children?
So noisy? So much at home they
must have been born in uniform
Lived all their lives in playgrounds
Spent the years inventing games
that don't let me in. Games
that are rough, that swallow you up.

And the railings.
All around, the railings.
Are they to keep out wolves and monsters?
Things that carry off and eat children?
Things you don't take sweets from?
Perhaps they're to stop us getting out
Running away from the lessins. Lessin.
What does a lessin look like?
Sounds small and slimy.
They keep them in glassrooms.
Whole rooms made out of glass. Imagine.

I wish I could remember my name
Mummy said it would come in useful.
Like wellies. When there's puddles.
Yellowwellies. I wish she was here.
I think my name is sewn on somewhere
Perhaps the teacher will read it for me.
Tea-cher. The one who makes the tea.

George and the Dragonfly

Georgie Jennings was spit almighty.
When the golly was good
he could down a dragonfly at 30 feet
and drown a 100 midges with the fallout.
At the drop of a cap
he would outspit lads
years older and twice his size.
Freckled and rather frail
he assumed the quiet dignity
beloved of schoolboy heroes.

But though a legend in his own playtime
Georgie Jennings failed miserably in the classroom
and left school at 15 to work for his father.
And talents such as spitting
are considered unbefitting
for upandcoming porkbutchers.

I haven't seen him since,
but like to imagine some summer soiree
when, after a day moistening mince,
George and his wife entertain tanned friends.
And after dinner, sherrytongued talk
drifts back to schooldays: the faces
halfrecalled, the adventures overexaggerated.

And the next thing,
that shy sharpshooter of days gone by
is led, vainly protesting, on to the lawn
where, in the hush of a golden august evening
a reputation, 20 years tall, is put to the test.

So he takes extra care as yesterheroes must,
fires, and a dragonfly, encapsulated, bites the dust.
Then amidst bravos and tinkled applause,
blushing, Georgie leads them back indoors.

The Horse's Mouth

They bought the horse
in Portobello
brought it home
could hardly wait
installed it in the living room
next to knitted dinner plate

Next to ashtray
(formerly bedpan)
euphonium
no one can play
camel-saddle dollypeg
wooden gollywog with tray

Near a neo
deco lampshade
(a snip at
thirty-seven quid)
castanets and hula-hoop
trunk with psychedelic lid

Under front end
of a caribou
next to foam-
filled rollerskate
(made by a girl in Camden Lock
– she of knitted dinner plate)

Uprooted from
its carousel
the painted horse
now laid to waste
amidst expensive bric-à-brac
and sterile secondhand bad taste

*   *   *

And each night as Mr and Ms Trend
in brassbed they lie dreaming
the horse in downstairs darkness
mouths a silent screaming.

The Lake

For years there have been no fish in the lake.
People hurrying through the park avoid it like the plague.
Birds steer clear and the sedge of course has withered.
Trees lean away from it, and at night it reflects,
not the moon, but the blackness of its own depths.
There are no fish in the lake. But there is life there.
There is life . . .

Underwater pigs glide between reefs of coral debris.
They love it here. They breed and multiply
in sties hollowed out of the mud
and lined with mattresses and bedsprings.
They live on dead fish and rotting things,
drowned pets, plastic and assorted excreta.
Rusty cans they like the best.
Holding them in webbed trotters
their teeth tear easily through the tin
and poking in a snout
they noisily suck out
the putrid matter within.

There are no fish in the lake. But there is life there.
There is life . . .

For on certain evenings after dark
shoals of pigs surface and look out
at those houses near the park.
Where, in bathrooms, children feed stale bread
  to plastic ducks. And in attics,
toyyachts have long since runaground.

Where, in livingrooms, anglers dangle their lines
on patterned carpets, and bemoan the fate
of the ones that got away.

Down on the lake, piggy eyes glisten.
They have acquired a taste for flesh.
They are licking their lips. Listen . . .

Crusader

in bed
like a dead
crusader

arms a
cross my chest
i lie

eyes closed
listening
to the bodys glib mechanics

*   *   *

on the street
outside
men of violence

quarrel.
Their drunken voices
dark weals

on the
glistening
back of the night.

There are Fascists

there are
fascists
pretending
to be
humanitarians

like
cannibals
on a health kick
eating only
vegetarians

Vegetarians

Vegetarians are cruel, unthinking people.
Everybody knows that a carrot screams when grated.
That a peach bleeds when torn apart.
Do you believe an orange insensitive
to thumbs gouging out its flesh?
That tomatoes spill their brains painlessly?
Potatoes, skinned alive and boiled,
the soil's little lobsters.
Don't tell me it doesn't hurt
when peas are ripped from the scrotum,
the hide flayed off sprouts,
cabbage shredded, onions beheaded.

Throw in the trowel
and lay down the hoe.
Mow no more
Let my people go!

There Was a Knock on the Door.
It Was the Meat.

There was a knock on the door.
It was the meat. I let it in.
Something freshly slaughtered
Dragged itself into the hall.

Into the living-room it crawled.
I followed. Though headless,
It headed for the kitchen
As if following a scent.

Straight to the oven it went
And lay there. Oozing softly to itself.
Though moved, I moved inside
And opened wide the door.

I switched to Gas Mark Four.
Set the timer. And grasping
The visitor by a stump
Humped it home and dry.

Did I detect a gentle sigh?
A thank you? The thought that I
Had helped a thing in need
Cheered me as I turned up the heat.

Two hours later the bell rang.
It was the meat.

Blazing Fruit

(or *The Role of the Poet as Entertainer*)

During dinner the table caught fire.
No one alluded to the fact
and we ate on, regardless of
the flames singeing our conversation.

Unaware of the smoke
and the butlers swooning,
topics ranged from Auden
to Zefferelli. I was losing
concentration however, and being
short on etiquette, became tense
and began to fidget with the melting cutlery.

I was fashioning a spoon
into a question mark
when the Chablis began to steam
and bubble. I stood up,
mumbled something about having left the gas running
and fled blushing
across the plush terrain of the carpet.

The tut-tut-tutting could be heard above
the cra-cra-cracking of the bone china.

Outside, I caught a cab
to the nearest bus stop.
While, back at the table,
they were toying with blazing fruit
and discussing the Role of the Poet as Entertainer,
when the roof fell in.

'Take a poem, Miss Smith.'

'Take a poem, Miss Smith.
I will call it *The Ploughman*.
"The ploughman wearily follows the plough,
The dust that lies upon his brow,
Gnarled as the dead oak tree bough,
Makes me think of how . . . of how . . ."
How nice you smell, Miss Smith.
Is it Chanel? I thought so.
But to work: "The ploughman wearily follows . . ."
Ah, but I am wearied of ploughing.
File it away under "Nature – unfinished".

'Take a poem, Miss Smith.
It is entitled *Ulster*.
"Along the Shankhill Road, a pall
Of smoke hangs, thick as . . . thick as . . ."
Hair, something different about the hair.
A new style? It suits you.
But where was I? Oh yes:
"Along the Shankhill Road . . ."
No, I feel unpolitical today.
Put it away in the file
marked "Wars – unfinished".

'Take a poem, Miss Smith.
It will be known as *Flesh*.
"The flesh I love to touch
Is soft as . . . soft as . . ."
Take off your blouse, Miss Smith,
I feel a love poem coming on . . .'

40 –

middle

couple

ten

when

game

and

go

the

will

be

tween

Love

aged

playing

nis

the

ends

they

home

net

still

be

them

You and I

I explain quietly. You
hear me shouting. You
try a new tack. I
feel old wounds reopen.

You see both sides. I
see your blinkers. I
am placatory. You
sense a new selfishness.

I am a dove. You
recognize the hawk. You
offer an olive branch. I
feel the thorns.

You bleed. I
see crocodile tears. I
withdraw. You
reel from the impact.

The Rot

Some years ago the Rot set in.
It began in a corner of the bedroom
following the birth of the second child.
It spread into the linen cupboard
and across the fabric of our lives.
Experts came to treat it.
Could not.
The Rot could not be stopped.

Dying now, we live with it.
The fungus grows.
It spreads across our faces.
We watch the smiles rot,
gestures crumble.
Diseased, we become the disease.
Part of the fungus.
The part that dreams. That feels pain.

We are condemned.
Things dying, that flaunt their dying,
that cannot hide, are demolished.
We will rot eachother no longer.
From the street outside
comes the sound of the drill,
as men, hungry for dust,
close in for the kill.

Mouth

I went to the mirror
but the mirror was bare,
looked for my mouth
but my mouth wasn't there.
Over the lips had grown
a whiskered hymen of skin.

I went to the window
wanting to shout
I pictured the words
but nothing came out.
The face beneath the nose
an empty hoarding.

And as I waited, I could feel
flesh filling in the space behind.
Teeth melted away tasting of snow
as the stalactites of the palate
joined the stalagmites below.
The tongue, like a salted snail,
sweated and shrivelled.

The doctor has suggested plastic surgery:
a neat incision, cosmetic dentistry
and full red lips (factory fresh).
He meant well but I declined.

After all, there are advantages.
At last I have given up smoking,
and though food is a needle
twice a day, it needs no cooking.

There is little that I miss.
I never could whistle and there's no one to kiss.

In the street, people pass by
unconcerned. I give no one directions
and in return am given none.
When asked if I am happy
I look the inquisitor straight in the eye
and think to myself . . . ('

Noah's Arc

In my fallout shelter I have enough food
For at least three months. Some books,
Scrabble, and games for the children.
Calor gas and candles. Comfortable beds
And a chemical toilet. Under lock and key
The tools necessary for a life after death.
I have carried out my instructions to the letter.

Most evenings I'm down here. Checking the stores,
Our suits, breathing apparatus. Cleaning
And polishing. My wife, bless her,
Thinks I'm obsessive – like other men
About cars or football. But deep down
She understands. I have no hobbies.
My sole interest is survival.

Every few weeks we have what I call D.D.,
Or Disaster Drill. At the sound of the alarm
We each go about our separate duties:
Disconnecting services, switching off the mains,
Filling the casks with fresh water, etc.
Mine is to oversee everything before finally
Shooting the dog. (This I mime in private.)

At first, the young ones enjoyed the days
And nights spent below. It was an adventure.
But now they're at a difficult age
And regard extinction as the boring concern
Of grown-ups. Like divorce and accountancy.
But I am firm. Daddy knows best
And one fine day they'll grow to thank me.

Beneath my bunk I keep an Armalite rifle
Loaded and ready to use one fine day
When panicking neighbours and so-called friends
Try to clamber aboard. The ones who scoff,
Who ignore the signs. I have my orders,
There will be no stowaways. No gatecrashers
At my party. A party starting soon.

And the sooner the better. Like a grounded
Astronaut I grow daily more impatient.
Am on tenterhooks. Each night
I ask the Lord to get on with it.
I fear sometimes He has forsaken us,
We His favourite children. Meek, drilled,
And ready to inherit an earth, newly-cleansed.

I scan the headlines, watch the screen.
A doctor thrilling at each fresh tumour:
The latest invasion, a breakdown of talks.
I pray for malignancy. The self-induced
Sickness for which there is only one cure:
Radium treatment. The final absolution.
That part of full circle we have yet to come.

The Identification

So you think its Stephen?
Then I'd best make sure
Be on the safe side as it were.
Ah, theres been a mistake. The hair
you see, its black, now Stephens fair . . .
Whats that? The explosion?
Of course, burnt black. Silly of me.
I should have known. Then lets get on.

The face, is that a face I ask?
That mask of charred wood
blistered, scarred could
that have been a child's face?
The sweater, where intact, looks
in fact all too familiar.
But one must be sure.

The scoutbelt. Yes thats his.
I recognize the studs he hammered in
not a week ago. At the age
when boys get clothes-conscious
now you know. Its almost
certainly Stephen. But one must
be sure. Remove all trace of doubt.
Pull out every splinter of hope.

Pockets. Empty the pockets.
Handkerchief? Could be any schoolboy's.
Dirty enough. Cigarettes?
Oh this can't be Stephen.
I dont allow him to smoke you see.
He wouldn't disobey me. Not his father.

But thats his penknife. Thats his alright.
And thats his key on the keyring
Gran gave him just the other night.
So this must be him.

I think I know what happened
. . .. about the cigarettes
No doubt he was minding them
for one of the older boys.
Yes thats it.
Thats him.
Thats our Stephen.

Head Injury

I do not smile because I am happy.
Because I gurgle I am not content.
I feel in colours, mottled, mainly black.
And the only sound I hear is the sea
Pounding against the white cliffs of my skull.

For seven months I lay in a coma.
Agony.
Darkness.
My screams drowned by the wind
Of my imperceptible breathing.

One morning the wind died down. I awoke.

You are with me now as you are everyday
Seeking some glimmer of recognition
Some sign of recovery. You take my hand.
I try to say: 'I love you.'
Instead I squawk,
Eyes bobbing like dead birds in a watertank.
I try to say: 'Have pity on me, pity on yourself
Put a bullet between the birds.'
Instead I gurgle.
You kiss me then walk out of the room.
I see your back.
I feel a colour coming, mottled, mainly black.

ROGER McGOUGH

Waving at Trains

Do people who wave at trains
Wave at the driver, or at the train itself?
Or, do people who wave at trains
Wave at the passengers? Those hurtling strangers,
The unidentifiable flying faces?

They must think we like being waved at.
Children do perhaps, and alone
In a compartment, the occasional passenger
Who is himself a secret waver at trains.
But most of us are unimpressed.

Some even think they're daft.
Stuck out there in a field, grinning.
But our ignoring them, our blank faces,
Even our pulled tongues and up you signs
Come three miles further down the line.

Out of harm's way by then
They continue their walk.
Refreshed and made pure, by the mistaken belief
That their love has been returned,
Because they have not seen it rejected.

It's like God in a way. Another day
Another universe. Always off somewhere.
And left behind, the faithful few,
Stuck out there. Alone in compartments.
All innocence. Arms in the air. Waving.

P.C. Plod at the Pillar Box

It's snowing out
streets are thiefproof
A wind that blows
straight up yer nose
no messin
A night
not fit to be seen with a dog
out in

On the corner
P.C. Plod (brave as a mountain lion)
passes the time of night
with a pillar box
'What's 7 times 8 minus 56?'
he asked mathematically
The pillar box was silent for a moment
and then said
nothing
'Right first time,'
said the snowcapped cop
and slouched off towards Bethlehem
Avenue

BRIAN PATTEN

Brian Patten was born in Liverpool in 1946. At fifteen he began publishing a magazine called *Underdog*. It was the first magazine to publish seriously many of the then underground poets, including Roger McGough and Adrian Henri, and it had a direct influence on the numerous broadsheets and magazines that followed.

Brian Patten's poetry and children's books are published in many languages, including Spanish, Dutch, Japanese, Polish and German. His collections of poetry include *Little Johnny's Confession*, *Notes to the Hurrying Man*, *The Irrelevant Song*, *Vanishing Trick*, *Grave Gossip* and *Love Poems*; his work has been widely anthologized and is included in *The Oxford Book of Twentieth-Century Verse*. His books for children are *The Elephant and the Flower*, *Jumping Mouse*, *The Sly Cormorant*, *Emma's Doll* and *Mr Moon's Last Case*, which has been hailed as a classic by reviewers in Britain and in the United States where it won a special award from the Mystery Writers of America Guild; and he edited *Gangsters, Ghosts and Dragonflies*. He has made several LPs, among them 'The Sly Cormorant', verse adaptations of *Aesop's Fables*, read by himself and Cleo Laine, with music by Brian Gascoigne. He has also written a number of plays, notably *The Pig and the Junkle*, a children's play which was commissioned by the Everyman Theatre in Liverpool, and, with Roger McGough, *The Mouthtrap*, which opened at the Edinburgh Festival in 1982 and transferred to the Lyric Theatre, Hammersmith.

A Blade of Grass

You ask for a poem.
I offer you a blade of grass.
You say it is not good enough.
You ask for a poem.

I say this blade of grass will do.
It has dressed itself in frost,
It is more immediate
Than any image of my making.

You say it is not a poem,
It is a blade of grass and grass
Is not quite good enough.
I offer you a blade of grass.

You are indignant.
You say it is too easy to offer grass.
It is absurd.
Anyone can offer a blade of grass.

You ask for a poem.
And so I write you a tragedy about
How a blade of grass
Becomes more and more difficult to offer,

And about how as you grow older
A blade of grass
Becomes more difficult to accept.

The Right Mask

One night a poem came to a poet.
From now on, it said, you must wear a mask.
What kind of mask? asked the poet.
A rose mask, said the poem.
I've used it already, said the poet,
I've exhausted it.
Then wear the mask that's made
Of the nightingale's song, use that mask.
But it's an old mask, said the poet,
It's all used up.
Nonsense! said the poem, it is the perfect mask.
Nevertheless, try on the God mask –
Now that mask illuminates Heaven.
But it is a tired mask, said the poet,
And the stars crawl about in it like ants.
Then try on the troubadour's mask, or the singer's mask,
Try on all the popular masks.
I have, said the poet, but they fit so awkwardly.
So try the mask of one beyond caring, said the poem,
Try the mask worn by one for whom
The night vomits up its secrets.
He shrugged the suggestion aside.
Now the poem was getting impatient,
It stamped its foot like a child. It screamed,
Then try on your own face!
Try on the one mask that terrifies you,
The mask no one else could possibly use,
The mask only you can wear out!
He tore at his face till it bled.
This mask? he asked, this mask?
Yes, said the poem, why not?
But he was tired even of that mask.

He had lived too long with it.
He tried to separate himself from it.
Its scream was muffled, it wept,
It tried to be lyrical.
It wriggled into his eyes and mouth,
Into his blood it wriggled.
The next day his friends did not recognize him,
They were afraid of him.
The mask was transparent.
Now it's the right mask, said the poem,
The right mask.
It clung to him lovingly,
And never let go again.

Friends

(for Liz Kylle and for Harry Fainlight)

I met them in bars and in railway stations
and I met them in borrowed rooms
and at bright gatherings,
and often enough
I met them with misgivings and doubts
and misinterpreted what they said
or did not understand at all
or understood so well
no explanations seemed needed.

And still, for all this, I kept on losing them.

And changes took place
and things that seemed extraordinary and out of reach
became life's most obvious gifts,
and the world slowed down, and I began
to meet them less and less.

Then I learned how the exodus from this place is not
    scheduled –
at times the young leave before the old and the old
are left gaping at their fortune.

And now Harry, you too are caught in your own
'miraculous stream that flows uphill'
caught in its flow toward Heaven,
and finally flesh has dropped away from memory,
and bald, bleak incidents are all I hold of you.

Looking through an address book containing
the names friends have abandoned
I realize that as from today
I haven't fingers enough to count
the graves in which they are exiled.

Someone Coming Back

Now that the summer has emptied
and laughter's warned against possessions,
and the swans have drifted from the rivers,
like one come back from a long journey
no longer certain of his country
or of its tangled past and sorrows,
I am wanting to return to you.

When love-affairs can no longer be distinguished from song
and the warm petals drop without regret,
and our pasts are hung in a dream of ruins,
I am wanting to come near to you.

From now the lark's song has grown visible
and all that was dark is ever possible
and the morning grabs me by the heart and screams,
'O taste me! Taste me please!'

And so I taste. And the tongue is nude,
the eyes awake; the clear blood hums
a tune to which the world might dance;
and love which often lived in vaguer forms
bubbles up through sorrow and laughing, screams:
'O taste me! Taste me please!'

Ode on Celestial Music

(or *It's The Girl In The Bathroom Singing*)

It's not celestial music it's the girl in the bathroom singing.
You can tell. Although it's winter
the trees outside her window have grown leaves,
all manner of flowers push up through the floorboards.
I think – 'what a filthy trick that is to play on me,'
I snip them with my scissors shouting
'I want only bona fide celestial music!'
Hearing this she stops singing.

Out of her bath now the girl knocks on my door,
'Is my singing disturbing you?' she smiles entering,
'did you say it was licentious or sensual?
And excuse me, my bath towel's slipping.'
A warm and blonde creature
I slam the door on her breasts shouting
'I want only bona fide celestial music!'

Much later on in life I wear my hearing-aid.
What have I done to my body, ignoring it,
splitting things into so many pieces my hands
cannot mend anything? The stars, the buggers, remained
silent.
Down in the bathroom now her daughter is singing.
Turning my hearing-aid full volume
I bend close to the floorboards hoping
for at least one song to get through.

A Few Sentences About Beauty

When something vanished from her face,
When something banished its first light
It left a puzzle there,
And I wanted to go to her and say,
'It is all imagining and will change,'
But that would have been too much a lie,
For beauty does reach some kind of height
And those who hunger for her now tomorrow might
Have a less keen appetite.
Yet beauty sinks deeper than the flesh,
And men seeking only surfaces will never know
What it is they have let go.

The Literary Gathering

In those rooms I became more distant than ever.
Where once I went with my head down,
Mumbling answers to obscure questions,
I felt a total stranger.

Poem-freak!
I felt I'd perverted imagination.
I had no real answers.
I'd left my brain at home preserved in lime.

Like a dumb canary let out of its cage
I'd found another cage.
It did not suit me.
In my beak the invitations melted.

Standing there I shook from sleep
What into sleep escaped.
I glanced around the books for friends,
Found only breasts dressed in the latest fashion.

Those for who I sang were not there,
But were instead outside, and laughing drunk
Climbed railings in some public park,
Not caring where it was they went.

Outside again I was alive again.
I begged my soul to be anonymous, to breathe
Free of obscure ambitions and the need
To explain away any song.

Her Song

For no other reason than I love him wholly
I am here; for this one night at least
The world has shrunk to a boyish breast
On which my head, brilliant and exhausted, rests,
And can know of nothing more complete.

Let the dawn assemble all its guilts, its worries
And small doubts that, but for love, would infect
This perfect heart.
I am as far beyond doubt as the sun.
I am as far beyond doubt as is possible.

Ghost Culture

The Minister kneeling on the floor hunched over
the home politics page slobbering
pink fingers counting the column inches given
his ghost-written speech on how best
to decapitate the landscape
the hostess
well-feathered house stuffed with finery
the little poet rasping out the tough sonnet
the morose social worker wearing
last year's most expensive fashion
as some kind of penance
the charming young publisher
the charmed financier
the nouveau poor sucking up the atmosphere
the black writer of revolutionary pamphlets
the priest holding forth from the plush armchair
on man's fall from paradise
glib mimic living in light's echo
the neat journalists
the purveyors of wound-cream
the high-class gossip merchants
the sour novelists
the past and present beauties
the landlords of Bedlam
the manipulators of ghost-culture
all history's goblins
agile among the contradictions
were stunned into an embarrassed silence
when from his pocket the guest of honour
produced a few crumpled and unexplained petals
and wept with exhaustion.

The True Confessions
of a Manuscript Sniffer

Deep down in the library vaults protected by verse-loving Dobermann Pinschers I stumbled upon the literary remains of William Wordsworth. What paradise deep in those pristine catacombs to fondle the remains of Emily Dickinson! To run cold and licentious eyes over the liquid prose of Virginia Woolf, to sniff, sick with passion, a bundle of mildewed underwear bequeathed by T. S. Eliot.

And what joy it was to tour those vaults where, by the stench of the still fresh air, I could tell I was among more recent acquisitions.

It was here I came upon the newly interred left eye of Robert Lowell, an eye that still blinked out in serious astonishment. And here in a special vault reserved for new mythologies I saw an exact replica of a Belsize Park gas oven, and in a jar next to it, preserved in brine, the tarry lungs of Auden wheezed on in exasperation. Here too I unearthed the mummified corpse of some long dead beauty; a tag around the throat informed me, 'About this creature much great poetry was written.'

And among the limbs and bloodless bits of human junk I discovered the greatest of all treasures: the decomposed kidneys of Dylan Thomas smuggled at great expense from a New York morgue. Thus does poetry survive in Academia.

Might I suggest in future
the bodies of all dying authors are wrapped in their manu-
scripts and frozen
and preserved in zoos and funfairs
so that the student of literature
might study under more realistic conditions
the state of the battered and bartered and lovely human soul.

The Likelihood

At some time or other the dust will change its mind.
It will cease to be dust.
It will start over again.
It will reconstitute itself,
become skin,
become a fingernail or perhaps
a heart beating slowly.
Whatever, let's keep our eyes open
in case we miss the moment
of the dust's rebellion,
and our ears open
for the small whisper of
'I'm fed up being dust,'   or
'I long to be an apple polished
against the sleeve
of a child I'd forgotten!'
It might be the dust buried beneath frost speaking,
or the dust of old machinery,
or the melancholic dust of friends
who believed in dying.
It might even be the dust of moths
God left uninvented.

Against a pile of such dust I have weighed
the likelihood of you returning.

It is Time to Tidy Up Your Life

It is time to tidy up your life!
Into your body has leaked this message.
No conscious actions, no broodings
Have brought the thought upon you.
It is time to take into account
What has gone and what has replaced it.
Living your life according to no plan
The decisions were numerous although
The ways to go were one.

You stand between trees this evening;
The cigarette in your cupped hand
Glows like a flower.
The drizzle falling seems
To wash away all ambition.
There are scattered through your life
Too many dreams to entirely gather.

Through the soaked leaves, the soaked grass,
The earth-scents and distant noises
This one thought is re-occurring:
It is time to take into account what has gone,
To cherish and replace it.
You learnt early enough that celebrations
Do not last forever,
So what use now the sorrows that mount up?

You must withdraw your love from that
Which would kill your love.
There is nothing flawless anywhere,
Nothing that has not the power to hurt.
As much as hate, tenderness is the weapon of one
Whose love is neither perfect nor complete.

January Gladsong

Seeing as yet nothing is really well enough arranged
the dragonfly will not yet sing
nor will the guests ever arrive
quite as naked as the tulips intended.
Still, because once again I am wholly glad of living,
I will make all that is possible step out of time
to a land of giant hurrays! where the happy monsters dance
and stomp darkness down.

Because joy and sorrow must finally unite and the small heart-
beat of sparrow be heard above jet-roar, I will sing
not of tomorrow's impossible paradise
but of what now radiates.
Forever the wind is blowing the white clouds in someone's
                                        pure direction.
In all our time birdsong has teemed and couples known
that darkness is not forever.
In the glad boat we sail the gentle and invisible ocean
where none have ever really drowned.

Simple Lyric

When I think of her sparkling face
And of her body that rocked this way and that,
When I think of her laughter,
Her jubilance that filled me,
It's a wonder I'm not gone mad.

She is away and I cannot do what I want.
Other faces pale when I get close.
She is away and I cannot breathe her in.

The space her leaving has created
I have attempted to fill
With bodies that numbed upon touching,
Among them I expected her opposite,
And found only forgeries.

Her wholeness I know to be a fiction of my making,
Still I cannot dismiss the longing for her;
It is a craving for sensation new flesh
Cannot wholly calm or cancel,
It is perhaps for more than her.

At night above the parks the stars are swarming.
The streets are thick with nostalgia;
I move through senseless routine and insensitive chatter
As if her going did not matter.
She is away and I cannot breathe her in.
I am ill simply through wanting her.

Interruption at the Opera House

At the very beginning of an important symphony,
while the rich and famous were settling into their quietly
                                       expensive boxes,
a man came crashing through the crowds,
carrying in his hand a cage in which
the rightful owner of the music sat,
yellow and tiny and very poor;
and taking onto the rostrum this rather timid bird
he turned up the microphones, and it sang.

'A very original beginning to the evening,' said the crowds,
quietly glancing at their programmes to find
the significance of the intrusion.

Meanwhile at the box office the organizers of the evening
were arranging for small and uniformed attendants
to evict, even forcefully, the intruders.
But as the attendants, poor and gathered from the nearby
                                       slums at little expense,
went rushing down the aisles to do their job
they heard, above the coughing and irritable rattling of jewels,
a sound that filled their heads with light,
and from somewhere inside them there bubbled up a stream,
and there came a breeze on which their youth was carried.
How sweetly the bird sang!

And though soon the fur-wrapped crowds
were leaving their boxes and in confusion were winding their
                                       way home
still the attendants sat in the aisles,
and some, so delighted at what they heard, rushed out to call
their families and friends.

And their children came,
sleepy for it was late in the evening,
very late in the evening,
and they hardly knew if they had done with dreaming
or had begun again.

In all the tenement blocks
the lights were clicking on,
and the rightful owner of the music,
tiny but no longer timid sang
for the rightful owners of the song.

Spring Song

I thought the tree was rather ordinary until yesterday
when seven girls in orange swim-wear climbed into its
                                                   branches.
Laughing and giggling they unstrapped each other,
letting their breasts fall out,
running fourteen nipples along the branches.
I sat at my window watching.
'Hey,' I said, 'what are yous doing up there?'
'We are coaxing out the small green buds earlier than usual,'
said the first.
Then the second slid down the tree – amazing how brown
                                                her body was –
and naked she lay on the dead clumpy soil for an hour or
                                                       more.
On rising there was a brilliant green shape of grass
and the beginning of daisies.

'Are you Spring?' I asked.
'Yes,' she replied. 'And the others also, they are Spring.'
I should have guessed.
What other season permits such nakedness?

The others came in through the window then.
All the dust the room had gathered vanished.
They are the happy gardeners;
their long backs bend to gather cartloads of sadness
and take it elsewhere.

They'll walk among us making our touch perfect.
Their beauty more awkward than even the topmost models,
they'll take our hearts to the laundry
and there'll be but joy in whatever rooms we wake.

We'll love all in that country
where couples glow brilliant
and the loneliest amongst them find in their bodies
a promise of laughter.

The Stolen Orange

When I went out I stole an orange
I kept it in my pocket
It felt like a warm planet

Everywhere I went smelt of oranges
Whenever I got into an awkward situation
I'd take the orange out and smell it

And immediately on even dead branches I saw
The lovely and fierce orange blossom
That smells so much of joy

When I went out I stole an orange
It was a safeguard against imagining
there was nothing bright or special in the world

Proclamation from the New Ministry of Culture

A festival is to be held during which
A competition is to be held during which
Work that exalts the free spirit of this land
May be submitted.
The judges can be chosen from among yourselves
The honours to be awarded are numerous,
The prizes to be awarded are numerous.
You may write or paint exactly what you wish,
You may say exactly what you wish
About the free spirit of this land.

Work in bad taste will be disqualified.
Anonymous entries will be ferreted out.
Those who do not enter will be considered
Enemies of the free spirit of this land.

From now on the festival is to be an annual event.

In the High Rise
Alice Dreams of Wonderland

She received a parcel through the post.
It had everything she wanted inside it.
Sometimes when she touched it
a planet-sized man would come to the door
and say exactly the right kind of thing.
The parcel kept her happy.
Provided all she needed.
Her children blossomed,
grew fat and pink and healthy.
The high-rise in which she lived shrank,
became a neat house –
a swing on the lawn, a driveway, etc.

A bill for the parcel arrived on Monday
On Tuesday came a reminder.
On Wednesday came a solicitor's letter.
On Thursday came a court order.
On Friday the jury gave a verdict.
On Saturday the parcel was taken.
Most days
Alice can be seen in the high-rise,
mouth twisted, weeping.

You Come to Me Quiet as Rain
Not Yet Fallen

You come to me quiet as rain not yet fallen
afraid of how you might fail yourself your
dress seven summers old is kept open
in memory of sex, smells warm, of boys,
and of the once long grass.
But we are colder now; we have not
love's first magic here. You come to me
quiet as bulbs not yet broken
out into sunlight.

The fear I see in your now lining face
changes to puzzlement when my hands reach
for you as branches reach. Your dress
does not fall easily, nor does your body
sing of its own accord. What love added to
a common shape no longer seems a miracle.
You come to me with your age wrapped in excuses
and afraid of its silence.

Into the paradise our younger lives made
of this bed and room
has leaked the world and all its questioning
and now those shapes terrify us most
that remind us of our own. Easier now
to check longings and sentiment,
to pretend not to care overmuch,
you look out across the years, and you come to me
quiet as the last of our senses closing.

Frogs in the Wood

How good it would be to be lost again,
Night falling on the compass and the map
Turning to improbable flames,
Bright ashes going out in the ponds.

And how good it would be
To stand bewildered in a strange wood
Where you are the loudest thing,
Your heart making a deafening noise.

And how strange when your fear of being lost has subsided
To stand listening to the frogs holding
Their arguments in the streams,
Condemning the barbarous herons.

And how right it is
To shrug off real and invented grief
As of no importance
To this moment of your life,

When being lost seems
So much more like being found,
And you find all that is lost
Is what weighed you down.

A Drop of Unclouded Blood

All day I will think of these cities floating fragile
across the earth's crust
and of how they are in need
of a drop of magic blood
a drop of unclouded blood

All day I will think of snow and the small
violets like a giant's blood
splashed at random on the earth
All day I will stroll about hoping
for a drop of unclouded blood
to fall into my veins

I need my body to move loose through the world
Need my fingers to touch the skin
of children adrift in their temporary world
Beneath their dreaming is a drop of blood
refusing the sun's heat
a drop of blood more pure than any other blood

I need to walk through the pale light
that occupies the world
and believe it when a drop of blood says
Listen,
paradise is never far away
and simpler than you think it

I need to sever all connection with the habits
that make the heart
love only certain things
I need a drop of magic blood for that
a drop of unclouded blood

Waves

And the one throwing the lifebelt,
Even he needs help at times,
Stranded on the beach,
Terrified of waves.

Albatross Ramble

I woke this morning to find an albatross staring at me.
Funny, it wasn't there last night.
Last night I was alone.

The albatross lay on the bed.
The sheets were soaking.

I live miles from any coast.
I invited no mad sailors home.
I dreamt of no oceans.

The bird is alive, it watches me carefully.
I watch it carefully.
For some particular reason I think
Maybe we deserve one another.

It's sunny outside, spring even.
The sky is bright; it is alive.

I remember I have someone to meet,
Someone clear, someone with whom I'm calm,
Someone who lets things glow.

As I put on my overcoat to go out
I think that maybe after all
I don't deserve this bird.

Albatrosses cause hang-ups.
There's not much I can do with them.
I can't give them in to zoos.
The attendants have enough albatrosses.

Nobody is particularly eager to take it from me.

Maybe, I think, the bird's in the wrong house.
Maybe it meant to go next door.
Maybe some sailor lives next door.
Maybe it belongs to the man upstairs.
Maybe it belongs to the girls in the basement.
It must belong to someone.

I rush into the corridor and shout:
'Does anyone own an albatross? Has anyone lost it?
There's an albatross in my room!'

I'm met by an awkward silence.

I know the man upstairs is not happy.
I know the girls in the basement wander lost among the
                                                    furniture.
Maybe they're trying to get rid of it
And won't own up.
Maybe they've palmed the albatross off on me.

I don't want an albatross; I don't want this bird;
I've got someone to meet,
Someone patient, someone good and healthy,
Someone whose hands are warm and whose grin
Makes everything babble and say yes.
I'd not like my friend to meet the albatross.

It would eat those smiles;
It would bother that patience;
It would peck at those hands
Till they turned sour and ancient.

Although I have made albatross traps,
Although I have sprayed the thing with glue,
Although I have fed it every poison available,
It still persists in living,
This bird with peculiar shadows
Cast its darkness over everything.

If I go out it would only follow.
It would flop in the seat next to me on the bus,
Scowling at the passengers.
If I took it to the park it would only bother the ducks,
Haunt couples in rowing boats,
Tell the trees it's winter.
It would be patted by policemen as they gently asked:
'Have you an albatross licence?'

Gloom bird, doom bird,
I can do nothing about it.
There are no albatross-exterminators in the directory;
I looked for hours.

Maybe it will stay with me right through summer;
Maybe it has no intentions of leaving.
I'll grow disturbed with this bird never leaving,
This alien bird with me all the time.

And now my friend is knocking on the door,
Less patient, frowning,
A bit sad and angry.

I'll sit behind this door and make noises like an albatross.
A terrible crying.
I'll put my mouth to the keyhole and wail albatross wails.
My friend will know then
I have an albatross in my room.
My friend will sympathize with me,
Go away knowing it's not my fault I can't open the door.

I'll wait here; I might devise some plan:
It's spring and everything is good but for this.
This morning I woke with an albatross in my room.
There's nothing much I can do about it until it goes away.

Sometimes It Happens

And sometimes it happens that you are friends and then
You are not friends,
And friendship has passed.
And whole days are lost and among them
A fountain empties itself.

And sometimes it happens that you are loved and then
You are not loved,
And love is past.
And whole days are lost and among them
A fountain empties itself into the grass.

And sometimes you want to speak to her and then
You do not want to speak,
Then the opportunity has passed.
Your dreams flare up, they suddenly vanish.

And also it happens that there is nowhere to go and then
There is somewhere to go,
Then you have bypassed
And the years flare up and are gone,
Quicker than a minute.

So you have nothing.
You wonder if these things matter and then
As soon as you begin to wonder if these things matter
They cease to matter,
And caring is past.
And a fountain empties itself into the grass.

Tristan, Waking in his Wood, Panics

Do not let me win again, not this time,
Not again. I've won too often and know
What winning is about. I do not want to possess;
I do not want to. I will not want you.

Every time a thing is won,
Every time a thing is owned,
Every time a thing is possessed,
It vanishes.

Only the need is perfect, only the wanting.
Tranquillity does not suit me;
I itch for disasters.

I know the seasons; I'm familiar with
Those things that come and go,
Destroy, build up, burn and freeze me.

I'm familiar with opposites
And taste what I can,
But still I stay starving.

It would be easy to blame an age,
Blame fashions that infiltrate and cause
What was thought constant to change.

But what future if I admitted to no dream beyond the one
From which I'm just woken?
Already in the wood the light grass has darkened.

Like a necklace of deaths the flowers hug the ground;
Their scents, once magically known,
Seem now irretrievable.

On Time For Once

I was sitting thinking of our future
and of how friendship had overcome
so many nights bloated with pain;

I was sitting in a room that looked on to a garden
and a stillness filled me,
bitterness drifted from me.

I was as near paradise as I am likely to get again.

I was sitting thinking of the chaos
we had caused in one another
and was amazed we had survived it.

I was thinking of our future
and of what we would do together,
and where we would go and how,

when night came
burying me bit by bit,
and you entered the room

trembling and solemn-faced,
on time for once.